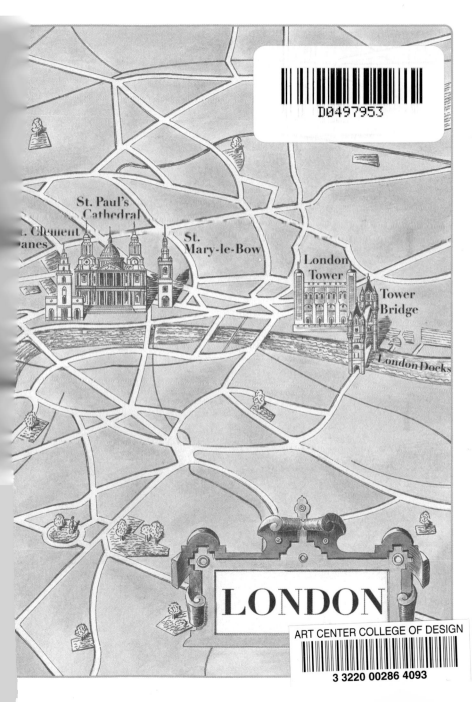

St. Paul's
Cathedral

t. Clement
Panes

St.
Mary-le-Bow

London
Tower

Tower
Bridge

London Docks

LONDON

THE LONDON SCENE

Six Essays on London Life

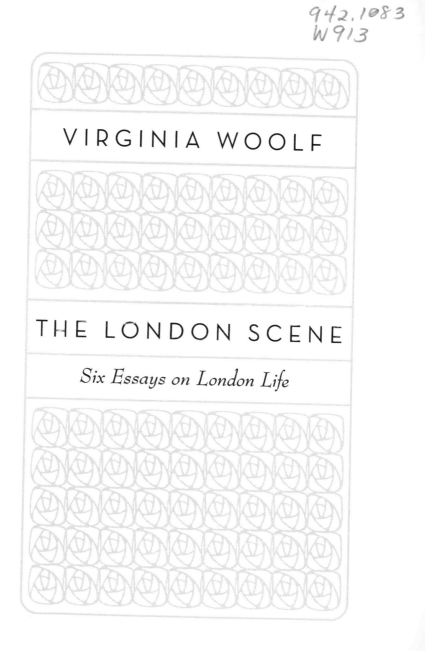

VIRGINIA WOOLF

THE LONDON SCENE

Six Essays on London Life

HarperCollins books may be purchased for educational, business, or sales promotional use. For information, please write: Special Markets Department, HarperCollins Publishers, 10 East 53rd Street, New York, NY 10022.

FIRST EDITION

Designed by Jessica Shatan Heslin
Endpaper map and illustrations by Rodica Prato

Printed on acid-free paper

Library of Congress Cataloging-in-Publication Data

Woolf, Virginia, 1882–1941.
The London scene : six essays on London life / Virginia Woolf.—1st ed.
p. cm.
ISBN-13: 978-0-06-088128-3 (acid-free paper)
ISBN-10: 0-06-088128-3 (acid-free paper)
1. London (England)—Description and travel. 2. London (England)—Social life and customs. I. Title.

DA684.W733 2006
942.1083—dc22   2005054170

06 07 08 09 10 ❖/RRD 10 9 8 7 6 5 4 3 2 1

"I love walking in London," said Mrs. Dalloway.
"Really it's better than walking in the country."

—Virginia Woolf, *Mrs. Dalloway* (1925)

CONTENTS

Introduction *by Francine Prose* ⊗ ix

The Docks of London ⊗ 3

Oxford Street Tide ⊗ 17

Great Men's Houses ⊗ 29

Abbeys and Cathedrals ⊗ 41

"This is the House of Commons" ⊗ 53

Portrait of a Londoner ⊗ 67

INTRODUCTION

by Francine Prose

AT THE OPENING OF *MRS. DALLOWAY*, ITS HEROINE sets out on her now famous errand: buying flowers for the evening's party. Crossing Victoria Street, she registers the sights and sounds swirling around her: "In people's eyes, in the swing, tramp, and trudge; in the bellow and the uproar; the carriages, motor cars, omnibuses, vans, sandwich men shuffling and swinging; brass bands, barrel organs; in the triumph and the jingle and the strange high singing of some aeroplane overhead was what she loved; life; London; this moment in June."

In the litany of what Clarissa Dalloway loves, London, it will be noted, follows directly after life itself, and before a moment in June.

Woolf herself felt much the same about the city where she was born, where she most enjoyed living, and for which she longed, often desperately, when she was obliged to leave it. "London," she wrote in her diary, "perpetually attracts, stimulates, gives me a play & a story & a poem, without any trouble, save that of moving my legs through the streets . . . To walk alone through London is the greatest rest."

To ask her, as the British edition of *Good Housekeeping* did in the spring of 1931, to write a series of bimonthly articles about London must have seemed like a natural assignment. And though Woolf complained about the tedium of correcting the essays, you can feel, percolating through them, her pleasure in being invited to respond directly to the cityscape around her in the essayistic way that is mostly precluded, in novels, by the necessity of keeping the narrative moving briskly along.

Just as one can tour contemporary Paris guided only by a volume of impressionist paintings, so *The London Scene* can still be used as a practical Baedeker to the city that Virginia Woolf so loved. Following her example, you can plot your route from the London docks to Oxford Street, from Westminster Abbey and the Houses of Parliament to the Carlyles' house in Chelsea.

Obviously, much has changed since Woolf wrote these six essays. German bombing devastated London in World War II, and postwar reconstruction and expansion notably altered the city's skyline, borders, and demographics. Like any living organism, London is constantly evolving, and, in these pages, Woolf monitors the rapidly changing streetscape: "But any day of the week one may see Oxford Street vanishing at the tap of a workman's pick as he stands perilously balanced on a dusty pinnacle knocking down walls and facades as if they were made of yellow cardboard and sugar icing." On the seedy Docklands waterfront that Woolf describes in the opening piece, luxury lofts and chic office buildings have replaced the "dingy, decrepit-looking warehouses" that "huddle on the land that has become flat and slimy with mud." The "one true Cockney," Mrs. Crowe, with her endless hunger for "a glorified version of village gossip," has doubtless been replaced by a very different sort of hostess, whose social appetites might need to be slaked by a different sort of urban gossip.

And yet like all great writers describing, and responding to, the city in which they lived—Balzac in Paris, Joyce in Dublin, Kafka in Prague, even Dostoyevsky in his quasi-phantasmagoric version of St. Petersburg—Woolf managed to capture something eternal and unchanging about London: its vivid bustle, its energy, its pride in its role as a center of commerce and culture, of government and godliness. She portrays, with unerring precision, the essence of the city's enduring landmarks and offers a mini-guide to its most celebrated churches, from St. Paul's ("Mind and body seem both to widen in this enclosure, to expand under this huge canopy where the light is neither daylight nor lamplight, but an ambiguous element, something between the two") to Westminster Abbey, where the dead buried beneath and behind its stones strike her as being engaged in perpetual conversation: "Everybody in the brilliant assembly has a mind and will of his own. The Abbey is shot with high-pitched voices; its peace is broken by emphatic gestures and characteristic attitudes. Not an inch of its walls but speaks and claims and illustrates." She advises the weary walker to steal a moment of tranquility in "those old graveyards which have become gardens and playgrounds," where the dead are actually quiet. And her avian description of the proceedings in the House of Commons could have been written yesterday: "They never alight for more than a few minutes: some are always flying off, others are always settling again. And from the flock rises the gabbling, the cawing, the croaking of a flock of birds, disputing merrily and with occasional vivacity over some seed, worm, or buried grain."

Woolf moves, characteristically, from the specific to the general. Her discussion of the reasons we might want to visit the houses of Keats and Carlyle, a chapter which happens to be my favorite, becomes a meditation on what draws us to, and what we expect from, the homes of our literary heroes. "We know them from their houses—it would seem to be a fact that writers stamp themselves upon their possessions more indelibly than other people. Of artistic taste they may have none; but they seem always to possess a much rarer and more interesting gift— a faculty for housing themselves appropriately, for making the table, the chair, the curtain, the carpet into their own image."

Ultimately, Woolf was a novelist, fascinated by character and by life even more than she was by buildings, streets, and institutions. And so her lost "Portrait of a Londoner" essay, rediscovered in 2004 by British publisher Emma Cahill in the University of Sussex archive, represents her effort to take us behind the facades of the homes we pass and to introduce us to the city as personified in a citizen we might otherwise not meet: "To know London not merely as a gorgeous spectacle, a mart, a court, a hive of industry, but as a place where people meet and talk, laugh, marry, and die, paint, write and act, rule and legislate, it was essential to know Mrs. Crowe."

Thus, in reading *The London Scene,* I am reminded once again how beautifully Woolf wrote, how gracefully, intelligently, and imaginatively, regardless of what she was writing: novels, essays, diaries, letters, and in his case, articles for *Good Housekeeping.* Every sentence rings clear; the book is full of sparkling phrases and passages we wish we had time to commit to memory, so that we might charm and bore our loved ones with them, on our next visit to London.

And so, while it might not list the hottest restaurants and the newest boutique hotels, *The London Scene* gives us an amalgam of intelligence and beauty that few, if any, guidebooks provide. I can't think of a single tourist handbook that offers you a sort of pipeline through which to hear the spirits of the dead poets chattering in Westminster Abbey, or the voice of Keats's house, "the voice of leaves brushing in the wind; of branches stirring in the garden." And no one can whisk us quite so entertainingly or so fast from the serenity of the poet's house to the clamor of the great city, of "London crowded and ribbed and compact, with its dominant domes, its guardian cathedrals; its chimneys and spires; its cranes and gasometers; and the perpetual smoke which no spring or autumn ever blows away. London has lain there time out of mind scarring that stretch of earth deeper and deeper, making it more uneasy, lumped and tumultuous, branding it for ever with an indelible scar. There it lies in layers, in strata, bristling and billowing with rolls of smoke ways caught on its pinnacles." Like the best traveling companion, Virginia Woolf clears away the smoke and shows us what lies beneath the layers and the strata of her city.

THE LONDON SCENE

Six Essays on London Life

THE DOCKS

OF LONDON

"WHITHER, O SPLENDID SHIP" THE POET ASKED AS he lay on the shore and watched the great sailing ship pass away on the horizon. Perhaps, as he imagined, it was making for some port in the Pacific; but one day almost certainly it must have heard an irresistible call and come past the North Foreland and the Reculvers, and entered the narrow waters of the Port of London, sailed past the low banks of Gravesend and Northfleet and Tilbury, up Erith Reach and Barking Reach and Gallion's Reach, past the gas works and the sewage works till it found, for all the world like a car on a parking ground, a space reserved for it in the deep waters of the Docks. There it furled its sails and dropped anchor.

However romantic and free and fitful they may seem, there is scarcely a ship on the seas that does not come to anchor in the Port of London in time. From a launch in midstream one can see them swimming up the river with all the marks of their voyage still on them. Liners come, high-decked, with their galleries and their awnings and their passengers grasping their bags and leaning over the rail, while the lascars tumble and scurry below—home they come, a thousand of these big ships every week of the year to anchor in the docks of London. They take their way majestically through a crowd of tramp steamers, and colliers and barges heaped with coal and swaying red sailed boats, which, amateurish though they look, are bringing bricks from Harwich or cement from Colchester—for all is business; there are no pleasure boats on this river. Drawn by some irresistible current, they come from the storms and calms of the sea, its silence and loneliness to their allotted anchorage. The engines stop; the sails are furled; and suddenly the gaudy funnels and the tall masts show up incongruously against a row of workmen's houses, against the black walls of huge warehouses. A curious change takes place. They have no longer the proper perspective of sea and sky behind them, and no longer the proper space in which to stretch their limbs. They lie captive, like soaring and winged creatures who have got themselves caught by the leg and lie tethered on dry land.

With the sea blowing its salt into our nostrils, nothing can be more stimulating than to watch the ships coming up the Thames—the big ships and the little ships, the battered and the splendid, ships from India, from Russia, from South America, ships from Australia coming from silence and danger and loneliness past us, home to harbour. But once they drop anchor, once the cranes begin their dipping and their swinging, it seems as if all romance were over. If we turn and go past the anchored ships towards London, we see surely the most dismal prospect in the world. The banks of the river are lined with dingy, decrepit-looking warehouses. They huddle on land that has become flat and slimy with mud. The same air of decrepitude and of being run up provisionally stamps them all. If a window is broken, broken it remains. A fire that has lately blackened and blistered one of them seems to have left it no more forlorn and joyless than its neighbours. Behind the masts and funnels lies a sinister dwarf city of workmen's houses. In the foreground cranes and warehouses, scaffolding and gasometers line the banks with a skeleton architecture.

When, suddenly, after acres and acres of this desolation one floats past an old stone house standing in a real field, with real trees growing in clumps, the sight is disconcerting. Can it be possible that there is earth, that there once were fields and crops beneath this desolation and disorder? Trees and fields seem to survive incongruously like a sample of another civilisation among the wall-paper factories and soap factories that have stamped out old lawns and terraces. Still more incongruously one passes an old grey country church which still rings its bells, and keeps its churchyard green as if country people were still coming across the fields to service. Further down, an inn with swelling bow windows still wears a strange air of dissipation and pleasure making. In the middle years of the nineteenth century it was a favourite resort of pleasure makers, and figured in some of the most famous divorce cases of the time. Now pleasure has gone and labour has come; and it stands derelict like some beauty in her midnight finery looking out over mud flats and candle works, while malodorous mounds of earth, upon which trucks are perpetually tipping fresh heaps, have entirely consumed the fields where, a hundred years ago, lovers wandered and picked violets.

As we go on steaming up the river to London we meet its refuse coming down. Barges heaped with old buckets, razor blades, fish tails, newspapers and ashes—whatever we leave on our plates and throw into our dust bins—are discharging their cargoes upon the most desolate land in the world. The long mounds have been fuming and smoking and harbouring innumerable rats and growing a rank coarse grass and giving off a gritty, acrid air for fifty years. The dumps get higher and higher, and thicker and thicker, their sides more precipitous with tin cans, their pinnacles more angular with ashes year by year. But then, past all this sordidity, sweeps indifferently a great liner, bound for India. She takes her way through rubbish barges, and sewage barges, and dredgers out to sea. A little further, on the left hand, we are suddenly surprised—the sight upsets all our proportions once more—by what appear to be the stateliest buildings ever raised by the hand of man. Greenwich Hospital with all its columns and domes comes down in perfect symmetry to the water's edge, and makes the river again a stately waterway where the nobility of England once walked at their ease on green lawns, or descended stone steps to their pleasure barges. As we come closer to the Tower Bridge the authority of the city begins to assert itself. The buildings thicken and heap themselves higher. The sky seems laden with heavier, purpler clouds. Domes swell; church spires, white with age, mingle with the tapering, pencil-

shaped chimneys of factories. One hears the roar and the reso-
nance of London itself. Here at last, we have landed at that thick
and formidable circle of ancient stone, where so many drums
have beaten and heads have fallen, the Tower of London itself.
This is the knot, the clue, the hub of all those scattered miles of
skeleton desolation and ant-like activity. Here growls and grum-
bles that rough city song that has called the ships from the sea
and brought them to lie captive beneath its warehouses.

Now from the dock side we look down into the heart of
the ship that has been lured from its voyaging and tethered
to the dry land. The passengers and their bags have disappeared;
the sailors have gone too. Indefatigable cranes are now at work,
dipping and swinging, swinging and dipping. Barrels, sacks,
crates are being picked up out of the hold and swung regularly
on shore. Rhythmically, dexterously, with an order that has
some aesthetic delight in it, barrel is laid by barrel, case by case,
cask by cask, one behind another, one on top of another, one
beside another in endless array down the aisles and arcades of
the immense low-ceiled, entirely plain and unornamented
warehouses. Timber, iron, grain, wine, sugar, paper, tallow,
fruit—whatever the ship has gathered from the plains, from the
forests, from the pastures of the whole world is here lifted from

its hold and set in its right place. A thousand ships with a thousand cargoes are being unladen every week. And not only is each package of this vast and varied merchandise picked up and set down accurately, but each is weighed and opened, sampled and recorded, and again stitched up and laid in its place, without haste, or waste, or hurry, or confusion by a very few men in shirt-sleeves, who, working with the utmost organisation in the common interest—for buyers will take their word and abide by their decision—are yet able to pause in their work and say to the casual visitor, "Would you like to see what sort of thing we sometimes find in sacks of cinnamon? Look at this snake!"

A snake, a scorpion, a beetle, a lump of amber, the diseased tooth of an elephant, a basin of quicksilver—these are some of the rarities and oddities that have been picked out of this vast merchandise and stood on a table. But with this one concession to curiosity, the temper of the Docks is severely utilitarian. Oddities, beauties, rarities may occur, but if so, they are instantly tested for their mercantile value. Laid on the floor among the circles of elephant tusks is a heap of larger and browner tusks than the rest. Brown they well may be, for these are the tusks of mammoths that have lain frozen in Siberian ice for fifty thousand years; but fifty thousand years are suspect in the eyes of the ivory expert. Mammoth ivory tends to warp; you cannot extract billiard balls from mammoths, but only umbrella handles and the backs of the cheaper kind of hand-glass. Thus if you buy an umbrella or a looking-glass not of the finest quality, it is likely that you are buying the tusk of a brute that roamed through Asian forests before England was an island.

One tusk makes a billiard ball, another serves for a shoehorn—every commodity in the world has been examined and graded according to its use and value. Trade is ingenious and indefatigable beyond the bounds of imagination. None of all the multitudinous products and waste products of the earth but has been tested and found some possible use for. The bales of wool that are being swung from the hold of an Australian ship are girt, to save space, with iron hoops; but the hoops do not litter the floor; they are sent to Germany and made into safety razors. The wool itself exudes a coarse greasiness. This grease, which is harmful to blankets, serves, when extracted, to make face cream. Even the burrs that stick in the wool of certain breeds of sheep have their use, for they prove that the sheep undoubtedly were fed on certain rich pastures. Not a burr, not a tuft of wool, not an iron hoop is unaccounted for. And the aptness of everything to its purpose, the forethought and readiness which have provided for every process, come, as if by the back door, to provide that element of beauty which nobody in the Docks has ever given half a second of thought to. The warehouse is perfectly fit to be a warehouse; the crane to be a crane. Hence beauty begins to steal in. The cranes dip and swing, and there is rhythm in their regularity. The warehouse walls are open wide to admit sacks and barrels; but through them one sees all the roofs of London, its masts and spires, and the unconscious, vigorous movements of men lifting and unloading. Because barrels of wine require to be laid on their sides in cool vaults all the mystery of dim lights, all the beauty of low arches is thrown in as an extra.

The wine vaults present a scene of extraordinary solemnity. Waving long blades of wood to which lamps have been fixed, we peer about, in what seems to be a vast cathedral, at cask after cask lying in a dim sacerdotal atmosphere, gravely maturing, slowly ripening. We might be priests worshipping in the temple of some silent religion and not merely wine tasters and Customs' Officers as we wander, waving our lamps up this aisle, down that. A yellow cat precedes us; otherwise the vaults are empty of all human life. Here side by side the objects of our worship lie swollen with sweet liquor, spouting red wine if tapped. A winy sweetness fills the vaults like incense. Here and there a gas jet flares, not indeed to give light, or because of the beauty of the green and grey arches which it calls up in endless procession, down avenue after avenue, but simply because so much heat is required to mellow the wine. Use produces beauty as a by-product. From the low arches a white cotton-wool-like growth depends. It is a fungus, but whether lovely or loathsome matters not; it is welcome because it proves that the air possesses the right degree of dampness for the health of the precious fluid.

Even the English language has adapted itself to the needs of commerce. Words have formed round objects and taken their exact outline. One may look in the dictionary in vain for the warehouse meaning of "valinch," "shrive," "shirt," and "flogger" but in the warehouse they have formed naturally on the tip of the tongue. So too the light stroke on either side of the barrel which makes the bung start has been arrived at by years of trial and experiment. It is the quickest, the most effective of actions. Dexterity can go no further.

The only thing, one comes to feel, that can change the routine of the docks is a change in ourselves. Suppose, for instance, that we gave up drinking claret, or took to using rubber instead of wool for our blankets, the whole machinery of production and distribution would rock and reel and seek about to adapt itself afresh. It is we—our tastes, our fashions, our needs—that make the cranes dip and swing, that call the ships from the sea. Our body is their master. We demand shoes, furs, bags, stoves, oil, rice puddings, candles; and they are brought us. Trade watches us anxiously to see what new desires are beginning to grow in us, what new dislikes. One feels an important, a complex, a necessary animal as one stands on the quayside watching the cranes hoist this barrel, that crate, that other bale from the holds of the ships that have come to anchor. Because one chooses to light a cigarette, all those barrels of Virginian tobacco are swung on shore. Flocks upon flocks of Australian sheep have submitted to the shears because we demand woollen overcoats in winter. As for the umbrella that we swing idly to and fro, a mammoth who roared through the swamps fifty thousand years ago has yielded up its tusk to make the handle.

Meanwhile the ship flying the Blue Peter moves slowly out of the dock; it has turned its bows to India or Australia once more. But in the Port of London, lorries jostle each other in the little street that leads from the dock—for there has been a great sale, and the cart horses are struggling and striving to distribute the wool over England.

OXFORD STREET

TIDE

Down in the Docks one sees things in their crudity, their bulk, their enormity. Here in Oxford Street they have been refined and transformed. The huge barrels of damp tobacco have been rolled into innumerable neat cigarettes laid in silver paper. The corpulent bales of wool have been spun into thin vests and soft stockings. The grease of sheep's thick wool has become scented cream for delicate skins. And those who buy and those who sell have suffered the same city change. Tripping, mincing, in black coats, in satin dresses, the human form has adapted itself no less than the animal product. Instead of hauling and heaving, it deftly opens drawers, rolls out silk on counters, measures and snips with yard sticks and scissors.

Oxford Street, it goes without saying, is not London's most distinguished thoroughfare. Moralists have been known to point the finger of scorn at those who buy there, and they have the support of the dandies. Fashion has secret crannies off Hanover Square, round about Bond Street, to which it withdraws discreetly to perform its more sublime rites. In Oxford Street there are too many bargains, too many sales, too many goods marked down to one and eleven three that only last week cost two and six. The buying and selling is too blatant and raucous. But as one saunters towards the sunset—and what with artificial light and mounds of silk and gleaming omnibuses, a perpetual sunset seems to brood over the Marble Arch—the garishness and gaudiness of the great rolling ribbon of Oxford Street has its fascination. It is like the pebbly bed of a river whose stones are for ever washed by a bright stream. Everything glitters and twinkles. The first spring day brings out barrows frilled with tulips, violets, daffodils in brilliant layers. The frail vessels eddy vaguely across the stream of the traffic. At one corner seedy magicians are making slips of coloured paper expand in magic tumblers into bristling forests of splendidly tinted flora—a subaqueous flower garden. At another, tortoises repose on litters of grass. The slowest and most contemplative of creatures display their mild activities on a foot or two of pavement, jealously guarded from passing feet. One infers that the desire of man for the tortoise, like the desire of the moth for the star, is a constant element in human nature. Nevertheless, to see a woman stop and add a tortoise to her string of parcels is perhaps the rarest sight that human eyes can look upon.

Taking all this into account—the auctions, the barrows, the cheapness, the glitter—it cannot be said that the character of Oxford Street is refined. It is a breeding ground, a forcing house of sensation. The pavement seems to sprout horrid tragedies; the divorces of actresses, the suicides of millionaires occur here with a frequency that is unknown in the more austere pavements of the residential districts. News changes quicker than in any other part of London. The press of people passing seems to lick the ink off the placards and to consume more of them and to demand fresh supplies of later editions faster than elsewhere. The mind becomes a glutinous slab that takes impressions and Oxford Street rolls off upon it a perpetual ribbon of changing sights, sounds and movement. Parcels slap and hit; motor omnibuses graze the kerb; the blare of a whole brass band in full tongue dwindles to a thin reed of sound. Buses, vans, cars, barrows stream past like the fragments of a picture puzzle; a white arm rises; the puzzle runs thick, coagulates, stops; the white arm sinks, and away it streams again, streaked, twisted, higgledy-piggledy, in perpetual race and disorder. The puzzle never fits itself together, however long we look.

On the banks of this river of turning wheels our modern aristocrats have built palaces just as in ancient days the Dukes of Somerset and Northumberland, the Earls of Dorset and Salisbury lined the Strand with their stately mansions. The different houses of the great firms testify to the courage, initiative, the audacity of their creators much as the great houses of Cavendish and Percy testify to such qualities in some faraway shire. From the loins of our merchants will spring the Cavendishes and Percys of the future. Indeed, the great Lords of Oxford Street are as magnanimous as any Duke or Earl who scattered gold or doled out loaves to the poor at his gates. Only their largesse takes a different form. It takes the form of excitement, of display, of entertainment, of windows lit up by night, of banners flaunting by day. They give us the latest news for nothing. Music streams from their banqueting rooms free. You need not spend more than one and eleven three to enjoy all the shelter that high and airy halls provide; and the soft pile of carpets, and the luxury of lifts, and the glow of fabrics, and carpets and silver. Percy and Cavendish could give no more. These gifts of course have an object—to entice the shilling and eleven pennies as freely from our pockets as possible; but the Percys and the Cavendishes were not munificent either without hope of some return, whether it was a dedication from a poet or a vote from a farmer. And both the old lords and the new added considerably to the decoration and entertainment of human life.

But it cannot be denied that these Oxford Street palaces are rather flimsy abodes—perhaps grounds rather than dwelling places. One is conscious that one is walking on a strip of wood laid upon steel girders, and that the outer wall, for all its florid stone ornamentation, is only thick enough to withstand the force of the wind. A vigorous prod with an umbrella point might well inflict irreparable damage upon the fabric. Many a country cottage built to house farmer or miller when Queen Elizabeth was on the throne will live to see these palaces fall into the dust. The old cottage walls, with their oak beams and their layers of honest brick soundly cemented together still put up a stout resistance to the drills and bores that attempt to introduce the modern blessing of electricity. But any day of the week one may see Oxford Street vanishing at the tap of a workman's pick as he stands perilously balanced on a dusty pinnacle knocking down walls and facades as lightly as if they were made of yellow cardboard and sugar icing.

And again the moralists point the finger of scorn. For such thinness, such papery stone and powdery brick reflect, they say, the levity, the ostentation, the haste and irresponsibility of our age. Yet perhaps they are as much out in their scorn as we should be if we asked of the lily that it should be cast in bronze, or of the daisy that it should have petals of imperishable enamel. The charm of modern London is that it is not built to last; it is built to pass. Its glassiness, its transparency, its surging waves of coloured plaster give a different pleasure and achieve a different end from that which was desired and attempted by the old builders and their patrons, the nobility of England. Their pride required the illusion of permanence. Ours, on the contrary, seems to delight in proving that we can make stone and brick as transitory as our own desires. We do not build for our descendants, who may live up in the clouds or down in the earth, but for ourselves and our own needs. We knock down and rebuild as we expect to be knocked down and rebuilt. It is an impulse that makes for creation and fertility. Discovery is stimulated and invention on the alert.

The palaces of Oxford Street ignore what seemed good to the Greeks, to the Elizabethan, to the eighteenth-century nobleman; they are overwhelmingly conscious that unless they can devise an architecture that shows off the dressing-case, the Paris frock, the cheap stockings, and the jar of bath salts to perfection, their palaces, their mansions and motor-cars and the little villas out at Croydon and Surbiton where their shop assistants live, not so badly after all, with a gramophone and wireless, and money to spend at the movies—all this will be swept to ruin. Hence they stretch stone fantastically; crush together in one wild confusion the styles of Greece, Egypt, Italy, America; and boldly attempt an air of lavishness, opulence, in their effort to persuade the multitude that here unending beauty, ever fresh, ever new, very cheap and within the reach of everybody, bubbles up every day of the week from an inexhaustible well. The mere thought of age, of solidity, of lasting for ever is abhorrent to Oxford Street.

Therefore if the moralist chooses to take his afternoon walk along this particular thoroughfare, he must tune his strain so that it receives into it some queer, incongruous voices. Above the racket of van and omnibus we can hear them crying. God knows, says the man who sells tortoises, that my arm aches; my chance of selling a tortoise is small; but courage! there may come along a buyer; my bed tonight depends on it; so on I must go, as slowly as the police allow, wheeling tortoises down Oxford Street from dawn till dusk. True, says the great merchant, I am not thinking of educating the mass to a higher standard of aesthetic sensibility. It taxes all my wits to think how I can display my goods with the minimum of waste and the maximum of effectiveness. Green dragons on the top of Corinthian columns may help; let us try. I grant, says the middle-class woman, that I linger and look and barter and cheapen and turn over basket after basket of remnants hour by hour. My eyes glisten unseemily I know, and I grab and pounce with disgusting greed. But my husband is a small clerk in a bank; I have only fifteen pounds a year to dress on; so here I come, to linger and loiter and look, if I can, as well dressed as my neighbours. I am a thief, says a woman of that persuasion, and a lady of easy virtue into the bargain. But it takes a good deal of pluck to snatch a bag from a counter when a customer is not looking; and it may contain only spectacles and old bus tickets after all. So here goes!

A thousand such voices are always crying aloud in Oxford Street. All are tense, all are real, all are urged out of their speakers by the pressure of making a living, finding a bed, somehow keeping afloat on the bounding, careless, remorseless tide of the street. And even a moralist, who is, one must suppose, since he can spend the afternoon dreaming, a man with a balance in the bank—even a moralist must allow that this gaudy, bustling, vulgar street reminds us that life is a struggle; that all building is perishable; that all display is vanity; from which we may conclude—but until some adroit shopkeeper has caught on to the idea and opened cells for solitary thinkers hung with green plush and provided with automatic glowworms and a sprinkling of genuine death's-head moths to induce thought and reflection, it is vain to try to come to a conclusion in Oxford Street.

GREAT MEN'S

HOUSES

LONDON, HAPPILY, IS BECOMING FULL OF GREAT men's houses, bought for the nation and preserved entire with the chairs they sat on and the cups they drank from, their umbrellas and their chests of drawers. And it is no frivolous curiosity that sends us to Dickens's house and Johnson's house and Carlyle's house and Keats's house. We know them from their houses—it would seem to be a fact that writers stamp themselves upon their possessions more indelibly than other people. Of artistic taste they may have none; but they seem always to possess a much rarer and more interesting gift— a faculty for housing themselves appropriately, for making the table, the chair, the curtain, the carpet into their own image.

Take the Carlyles, for instance. One hour spent in 5 Cheyne Row will tell us more about them and their lives than we can learn from all the biographies. Go down into the kitchen. There, in two seconds, one is made acquainted with a fact that escaped the attention of Froude, and yet was of incalculable importance—they had no water laid on. Every drop that the Carlyles used—and they were Scots, fanatical in their cleanliness—had to be pumped by hand from a well in the kitchen. There is the well at this moment and the pump and the stone trough into which the cold water trickled. And here, too, is the wide and wasteful old grate upon which all kettles had to be boiled if they wanted a hot bath; and here is the cracked yellow tin bath, so deep and so narrow, which had to be filled with the cans of hot water that the maid first pumped and then boiled and then carried up three flights of stairs from the basement.

The high old house without water, without electric light, without gas fires, full of books and coal smoke and four-poster beds and mahogany cupboards, where two of the most nervous and exacting people of their time lived, year in year out, was served by one unfortunate maid. All through the mid-Victorian age the house was necessarily a battlefield where daily, summer and winter, mistress and maid fought against dirt and cold for cleanliness and warmth. The stairs, carved as they are and wide and dignified, seem worn by the feet of harassed women carrying tin cans. The high panelled rooms seem to echo with the sound of pumping and the swish of scrubbing. The voice of the house—and all houses have voices—is the voice of pumping and scrubbing, of coughing and groaning. Up in the attic under a skylight Carlyle groaned, as he wrestled with his history, on a horsehair chair, while a yellow shaft of London light fell upon his papers and the rattle of a barrel organ and the raucous shouts of street hawkers came through walls whose double thickness distorted but by no means excluded the sound. And the season of the house—for every house has its season—seems to be always the month of February, when cold and fog are in the street and torches flare and the rattle of wheels grows suddenly loud and dies away. February after February Mrs. Carlyle lay coughing in the large four-poster hung with maroon curtains in which she was born, and as she coughed the many problems of the incessant battle, against dirt, against cold, came before her. The horsehair couch needed recovering; the drawing-room paper with its small, dark pattern needed cleaning; the yellow varnish on the panels was cracked and peeling—all must be stitched, cleansed, scoured with her own hands; and had she, or had she not, demolished the bugs that bred and bred in the ancient wood panelling? So the long watches of the sleepless night passed, and then she heard Mr. Carlyle stir above her, and held her breath and wondered if Helen were up and had lit the fire and heated the water for his shaving. Another day had dawned and the pumping and the scrubbing must begin again.

Thus number 5 Cheyne Row is not so much a dwelling-place as a battlefield—the scene of labour, effort and perpetual struggle. Few of the spoils of life—its graces and its luxuries— survive to tell us that the battle was worth the effort. The relics of drawing-room and study are like the relics picked up on other battlefields. Here is a packet of old steel nibs; a broken clay pipe; a pen-holder such as schoolboys use; a few cups of white and gold china, much chipped; a horsehair sofa and a yellow tin bath. Here, too, is a cast of the thin worn hands that worked here; and of the excruciated and ravished face of Carlyle when his life was done and he lay dead here. Even the garden at the back of the house seems to be not a place of rest and recreation, but another smaller battlefield marked with a tombstone beneath which a dog lies buried. By pumping and by scrubbing, days of victory, evenings of peace and splendour were won, of course. Mrs. Carlyle sat, as we see from the picture, in a fine silk dress, in a chair pulled up to a blazing fire and had everything seemly and solid about her; but at what cost had she won it! Her cheeks are hollow; bitterness and suffering mingle in the half-tender, half-tortured expression of the eyes. Such is the effect of a pump in the basement and a yellow tin bath up three pairs of stairs. Both husband and wife had genius; they loved each other; but what can genius and love avail against bugs and tin baths and pumps in the basement?

It is impossible not to believe that half their quarrels might have been spared and their lives immeasurably sweetened if only number 5 Cheyne Row had possessed, as the house agents put it, bath, h. and c., gas fires in the bedrooms, all modern conveniences and indoor sanitation. But then, we reflect, as we cross the worn threshold, Carlyle with hot water laid on would not have been Carlyle; and Mrs. Carlyle without bugs to kill would have been a different woman from the one we know.

An age seems to separate the house in Chelsea where the Carlyles lived from the house in Hampstead which was shared by Keats and Brown and the Brawnes. If houses have their voices and places their seasons, it is always spring in Hampstead as it is always February in Cheyne Row. By some miracle, too, Hampstead has always remained not a suburb or a piece of antiquity engulfed in the modern world, but a place with a character peculiar to itself. It is not a place where one makes money, or goes when one has money to spend. The signs of discreet retirement are stamped on it. Its houses are neat boxes such as front the sea at Brighton with bow windows and balconies and deck chairs on verandahs. It has style and intention as if designed for people of modest income and some leisure who seek rest and recreation. Its prevailing colours are the pale pinks and blues that seem to harmonise with the blue sea and the white sand; and yet there is an urbanity in the style which proclaims the neighbourhood of a great city. Even in the twentieth century this serenity still pervades the suburb of Hampstead. Its bow windows still look out upon vales and trees and ponds and barking dogs and couples sauntering arm in arm and pausing, here on the hill-top, to look at the distant domes and pinnacles of London, as they sauntered and paused and looked when Keats lived here. For Keats lived up the lane in a little white house behind wooden palings. Nothing has been much changed since his day. But as we enter the house in which Keats lived some mournful shadow seems to fall across the garden. A tree has fallen and lies propped. Waving branches cast their shadows up and down over the flat white walls of the house. Here, for all the gaiety and serenity of the neighbourhood, the nightingale sang; here, if anywhere, fever and anguish had their dwelling and paced this little green plot oppressed with the sense of quick-coming death and the shortness of life and the passion of love and its misery.

Yet if Keats left any impress upon his house it is the impression not of fever, but of that clarity and dignity which come from order and self-control. The rooms are small but shapely; downstairs the long windows are so large that half the wall seems made of light. Two chairs turned together are close to the window as if someone had sat there reading and had just got up and left the room. The figure of the reader must have been splashed with shade and sun as the hanging leaves stirred in the breeze. Birds must have hopped close to his foot. The room is empty save for the two chairs, for Keats had few possessions, little furniture and not more, he said, than one hundred and fifty books. And perhaps it is because the rooms are so empty and furnished rather with light and shadow than with chairs and tables that one does not think of people, here where so many people have lived. The imagination does not evoke scenes. It does not strike one that there must have been eating and drinking here; people must have come in and out; they must have put down bags, left parcels; they must have scrubbed and cleaned and done battle with dirt and disorder and carried cans of water from the basement to the bedrooms. All the traffic of life is silenced. The voice of the house is the voice of leaves brushing in the wind; of branches stirring in the garden. Only one presence—that of Keats himself—dwells here. And even he, though his picture is on every wall, seems to come silently, on the broad shafts of light, without body or footfall. Here he sat on the chair in the window and listened without moving, and saw without starting, and turned the page without haste though his time was so short.

There is an air of heroic equanimity about the house in spite of the death masks and the brittle yellow wreaths and the other grisly memorials which remind us that Keats died young and unknown and in exile. Life goes on outside the window. Behind this calm, this rustling of leaves, one hears the far-off rattle of wheels, the bark of dogs fetching and carrying sticks from the pond. Life goes on outside the wooden paling. When we shut the gate upon the grass and the tree where the nightingale sang we find, quite rightly, the butcher delivering his meat from a small red motor van at the house next door. If we cross the road, taking care not to be cut down by some rash driver—for they drive at a great pace down these wide streets—we shall find ourselves on top of the hill and beneath shall see the whole of London lying below us. It is a view of perpetual fascination at all hours and in all seasons. One sees London as a whole—London crowded and ribbed and compact, with its dominant domes, its guardian cathedrals; its chimneys and spires; its cranes and gasometers; and the perpetual smoke which no spring or autumn ever blows away. London has lain there time out of mind scarring that stretch of earth deeper and deeper, making it more uneasy, lumped and tumultuous, branding it for ever with an indelible scar. There it lies in layers, in strata, bristling and billowing with rolls of smoke always caught on its pinnacles. And yet from Parliament Hill one can see, too, the country beyond. There are hills on the further side in whose woods birds are singing, and some stoat or rabbit pauses, in dead silence, with paw lifted to listen intently to rustlings among the leaves. To look over London from this hill Keats came and Coleridge and Shakespeare, perhaps. And here at this very moment the usual young man sits on an iron bench clasping to his arms the usual young woman.

ABBEYS AND CATHEDRALS

It is a commonplace, but we cannot help repeating it, that St. Paul's dominates London. It swells like a great grey bubble from a distance; it looms over us, huge and menacing, as we approach. But suddenly St. Paul's vanishes. And behind St. Paul's, beneath St. Paul's, round St. Paul's when we cannot see St. Paul's, how London has shrunk! Once there were colleges and quadrangles and monasteries with fish ponds and cloisters; and sheep grazing on the greensward; and inns where great poets stretched their legs and talked at their ease. Now all this space has shrivelled. The fields are gone and the fish ponds and the cloisters; even men and women seem to have shrunk and become multitudinous and minute instead of single and substantial. Where Shakespeare and Jonson once fronted each other and had their talk out, a million Mr. Smiths and Miss Browns scuttle and hurry, swing off omnibuses, dive into tubes. They seem too many, too minute, too like each other to have each a name, a character, a separate life of their own.

If we leave the street and step into a city church, the space that the dead enjoy compared with what the living now enjoy, is brought home to us. In the year 1737 a man called Howard died and was buried in St. Mary-le-Bow. A whole wall is covered with the list of his virtues. "He was blessed with a sound and intelligent mind which shone forth conspicuously in the habitual exercise of great and godlike virtues. . . . In the midst of a profligate age he was inviolably attached to justice, sincerity and truth." He occupies space that might serve almost for an office and demand a rent of many hundreds a year. In our day a man of equal obscurity would be allotted one slice of white stone of the regulation size among a thousand others and his great and godlike virtues would have to go unrecorded. Again, in St. Mary-le-Bow all posterity is asked to pause and rejoice that Mrs. Mary Lloyd "closed an exemplary and spotless life" without suffering and indeed without regaining consciousness, aged 79 years.

Pause, reflect, admire, take heed of your ways—so these ancient tablets are always advising and exhorting us. One leaves the church marvelling at the spacious days when unknown citizens could occupy so much room with their bones and confidently request so much attention for their virtues when we— behold how we jostle and skip and circumvent each other in the street, how sharply we cut corners, how nimbly we skip beneath motor cars. The mere process of keeping alive needs all our energy. We have no time, we were about to say, to think about life or death either, when suddenly we run against the enormous walls of St. Paul's. Here it is again, looming over us, mountainous, immense, greyer, colder, quieter than before. And directly we enter we undergo that pause and expansion and release from hurry and effort which it is in the power of St. Paul's, more than any other building in the world, to bestow.

Something of the splendour of St. Paul's lies simply in its vast size, in its colourless serenity. Mind and body seem both to widen in this enclosure, to expand under this huge canopy where the light is neither daylight nor lamplight, but an ambiguous element something between the two. One window shakes down a broad green shaft; another tinges the flagstones beneath a cool, pale purple. There is space for each broad band of light to fall smoothly. Very large, very square, hollow-sounding, echoing with a perpetual shuffling and booming, the Cathedral is august in the extreme; but not in the least mysterious. Tombs heaped like majestic beds lie between the pillars. Here is the dignified reposing room to which great statesmen and men of action retire, robed in all their splendour, to accept the thanks and applause of their fellow-citizens. They still wear their stars and garters, their emblems of civic pomp and military pride. Their tombs are clean and comely. No rust or stain has been allowed to spot them. Even Nelson looks a little smug. Even the contorted and agonised figure of John Donne, wrapped in the marble twists of his grave clothes, looks as if it had left the stonemason's yard but yesterday. Yet it has stood here in its agony for three hundred years and has passed through the flames of the Fire of London. But death and the corruption of death are forbidden to enter. Here civic virtue and civic greatness are ensconced securely. True, a heavy bossed door has above it the legend that through the gate of death we pass to our joyful resurrection; but somehow the massive portals suggest that they open not upon fields of amaranth and moly where harps sound and heavenly choirs sing, but upon flights of marble steps that lead on to solemn council chambers and splendid halls, loud with trumpets and hung with banners. Effort and agony and ecstasy have no place in this majestic building.

No contrast could be greater than that between St. Paul's and Westminster Abbey. Far from being spacious and serene, the Abbey is narrow and pointed, worn, restless and animated. One feels as if one had stepped from the democratic helter skelter, the hubbub and hum-drum of the street, into a brilliant assembly, a select society of men and women of the highest distinction. The company seems to be in full conclave. Gladstone starts forward and then Disraeli. From every corner, from every wall, somebody leans or listens or bends forward as if about to speak. The recumbent even seem to lie attentive, as if to rise next minute. Their hands nervously grasp their sceptres, their lips are compressed for a fleeting silence, their eyes lightly closed as if for a moment's thought. These dead, if dead they are, have lived to the full. Their faces are worn, their noses high, their cheeks hollowed. Even the stone of the old columns seems rubbed and chafed by the intensity of the life that has been fretting it all these centuries. Voice and organ vibrate wirily among the chasings and intricacies of the roof. The fine fans of stone that spread themselves to make a ceiling seem like bare boughs withered of all their leaves and about to toss in the wintry gale. But their austerity is beautifully softened. Lights and shadows are changing and conflicting every moment. Blue, gold and violet pass, dappling, quickening, fading. The grey stone, ancient as it is, changes like a live thing under the incessant ripple of changing light.

Thus the Abbey is no place of death and rest; no reposing-room where the virtuous lie in state to receive the rewards of virtue. Is it, indeed, through their virtues that these dead have come here? Often they have been violent; they have been vicious. Often it is only the greatness of their birth that has exalted them. The Abbey is full of Kings and Queens, Dukes and Princes. The light falls upon gold coronets, and gold still lingers in the folds of ceremonial robes. Reds and yellows still blazon coats of arms and lions and unicorns. But it is full also of another and even more potent royalty. Here are the dead poets, still musing, still pondering, still questioning the meaning of existence. "Life is a jest and all things show it. I thought so once, and now I know it," Gay laughs. Chaucer, Spenser, Dryden and the rest still seem to listen with all their faculties on the alert as the clean-shaven clergyman in his spick-and-span red-and-white robes intones for the millionth time the commands of the Bible. His voice rings ripely, authoritatively through the building, and if it were not irreverent one might suppose that Gladstone and Disraeli were about to put the statement just propounded—that children should honour their parents—to the vote. Everybody in this brilliant assembly has a mind and a will of his own. The Abbey is shot with high-pitched voices; its peace is broken by emphatic gestures and characteristic attitudes. Not an inch of its walls but speaks and claims and illustrates. Kings and Queens, poets and statesmen still act their parts and are not suffered to turn quietly to dust. Still in animated debate they rise above the flood and waste of average human life, with their fists clenched and their lips parted, with an orb in one hand, a sceptre in another, as if we had forced them to rise on our behalf and testify that human nature can now and then exalt itself above the hum-drum democratic disorder of the hurrying street. Arrested, transfixed, there they stand suffering a splendid crucifixion.

Where then can one go in London to find peace and the assurance that the dead sleep and are at rest? London, after all, is a city of tombs. But London nevertheless is a city in the full tide and race of human life. Even St. Clement Danes—that venerable pile planted in the mid-stream of the Strand—has been docked of all those peaceful perquisites—the weeping trees, the waving grasses that the humblest village church enjoys by right. Omnibuses and vans have long since shorn it of these dues. It stands, like an island, with only the narrowest rim of pavement to separate it from the sea. And moreover, St. Clement Danes has its duties to the living. As likely as not it is participating vociferously, stridently, with almost frantic joy, but hoarsely as if its tongue were rough with the rust of centuries, in the happiness of two living mortals. A wedding is in progress. All down the Strand St. Clement Danes roars its welcome to the bridegroom in tail coat and grey trousers; to the bridesmaids virginal in white; and finally to the bride herself whose car draws up to the porch, and out she steps and passes undulating with a flash of white finery into the inner gloom to make her marriage vows to the roar of omnibuses, while outside the pigeons, alarmed, sweep in circles, and Gladstone's statue is crowded, like a rock with gulls, with nodding, waving, enthusiastic sightseers.

The only peaceful places in the whole city are perhaps those old graveyards which have become gardens and playgrounds. The tombstones no longer serve to mark the graves, but line the walls with their white tablets. Here and there a finely sculptured tomb plays the part of garden ornament. Flowers light up the turf, and there are benches under the trees for mothers and nursemaids to sit on, while the children bowl hoops and play hopscotch in safety. Here one might sit and read *Pamela* from cover to cover. Here one might drowse away the first days of spring or the last days of autumn without feeling too keenly the stir of youth or the sadness of old age. For here the dead sleep in peace, proving nothing, testifying nothing, claiming nothing save that we shall enjoy the peace that their old bones provide for us. Unreluctantly they have given up their human rights to separate names or peculiar virtues. But they have no cause for grievance. When the gardener plants his bulbs or sows his grass they flower again and spread the ground with green and elastic turf. Here mothers and nursemaids gossip; children play; and the old beggar, after eating his dinner from a paper bag, scatters crumbs to the sparrows. These garden graveyards are the most peaceful of our London sanctuaries and their dead the quietest.

"THIS IS THE HOUSE OF COMMONS"

OUTSIDE THE HOUSE OF COMMONS STAND the statues of great statesmen, black and sleek and shiny as sea lions that have just risen from the water. And inside the Houses of Parliament, in those windy, echoing halls, where people are for ever passing and repassing, taking green cards from policemen, asking questions, staring, accosting members, trooping at the heels of schoolmasters, nodding and laughing and running messages and hurrying through swing doors with papers and attache cases and all the other emblems of business and haste— here, too, are statues—Gladstone, Granville, Lord John Russell— white statues, gazing from white eyes at the old scenes of stir and bustle in which, not so very long ago, they played their part.

There is nothing venerable or time-worn, or musical, or ceremonious here. A raucous voice bawling "The Speaker!" heralds the tramp of a plain democratic procession whose only pomp is provided by the mace and the Speaker's wig and gown and gold badges of the head waiters. The raucous voice bawls again, "Hats off, Strangers!" upon which a number of dingy felt hats are flourished obediently and the head waiters bow from the middle downwards. That is all. And yet the bawling voice, the black gown, the tramp of feet on the stone, the mace and the dingy felt hats somehow suggest, better than scarlet and trumpets, that the Commons are taking their seats in their own House to proceed with the business of governing their own country. Vague though our history may be, we somehow feel that we common people won this right centuries ago, and have held it for centuries past, and the mace is our mace and the Speaker is our speaker and we have no need of trumpeters and gold and scarlet to usher our representative into our own House of Commons.

Certainly our own House of Commons from inside is not in the least noble or majestic or even dignified. It is as shiny and as ugly as any other moderate-sized public hall. The oak, of course, is grained yellow. The windows, of course, are painted with ugly coats of arms. The floor, of course, is laid with strips of red matting. The benches, of course, are covered with serviceable leather. Wherever one looks one says, "of course." It is an untidy, informal-looking assembly. Sheets of white paper seem to be always fluttering to the floor. People are always coming in and out incessantly. Men are whispering and gossiping and cracking jokes over each other's shoulders. The swing doors are perpetually swinging. Even the central island of control and dignity where the Speaker sits under his canopy, is a perching ground for casual members who seem to be taking a peep at the proceedings at their ease. Legs rest on the edge of the table where the mace lies suspended; and the secrets which repose in the two brass-bound chests on either side of the table are not immune from the prod of an occasional toe. Dipping and rising, moving and settling, the Commons remind one of a flock of birds settling on a stretch of ploughed land. They never alight for more than a few minutes; some are always flying off, others are always settling again. And from the flock rises the gabbling, the cawing, the croaking of a flock of birds, disputing merrily and with occasional vivacity over some seed, worm, or buried grain.

One has to say to oneself severely, "But this is the House of Commons. Here the destinies of the world are altered. Here Gladstone fought, and Palmerston and Disraeli. It is by these men that we are governed. We obey their orders every day of the year. Our purses are at their mercy. They decide how fast we shall drive our cars in Hyde Park; also whether we shall have war or peace." But we have to remind ourselves; for to look at they do not differ much from other people. The standard of dress is perhaps rather high. We look down upon some of the glossiest top hats still to be seen in England. A magnificent scarlet buttonhole blazes here and there. Everybody has been well fed and given a good education doubtless. But what with their chatter and laughter, their high spirits, and impatience and irreverence, they are not a whit more judicious, or more dignified, or more respectable-looking than any other assembly of citizens met to debate parish business or give prizes for fat oxen. This is true; but after a time some curious difference makes itself suspected. We feel that the Commons is a body of a certain character; it has been in existence for a long time; it has its own laws and licences. It is irreverent in a way of its own; and so, presumably, reverent too in its own way. It has somehow a code of its own. People who disregard this code will be unmercifully chastened; those who are in accord with it will be easily condoned. But what it condemns and what it condones, only those who are in the secret of the House can say. All we can be sure of is that a secret there is. Perched up high as we are, under the rule of an official who follows the prevailing informality by crossing his legs and scribbling notes on his knee, we feel sure that nothing could be easier than to say the wrong thing, either with the wrong levity or the wrong seriousness, and that no assurance of virtue, genius, valour is here sure of success if something else —some indefinable quality—is omitted.

But how, one asks, remembering Parliament Square, are any of these competent, well-groomed gentlemen going to turn into statues? For Gladstone, for Pitt, or for Palmerston even, the transition was perfectly easy. But look at Mr. Baldwin—he has all the look of a country gentleman poking pigs; how is he going to mount a plinth and wrap himself decorously in a towel of black marble? No statue that did not render the shine of Sir Austen's top hat could do justice to him. Mr. Henderson seems constitutionally opposed to the pallor and severity of marble. As he stands there answering questions his fair complexion flushes scarlet, and his yellow hair seems to have been sleeked down with a wet brush ten minutes ago. Sir William Jowitt, it is true, might, if one took off his spruce bow tie, sit to some sculptor for a bust much in the style of the Prince Consort. Ramsay MacDonald has "features," as the photographers say, and could fill a marble chair in a public square without looking conspicuously ridiculous. But for the rest, the transition into marble is unthinkable. Mobile, irreverent, commonplace, snub-nosed, red-jowled, squires, lawyers, men of business—their prime quality, their enormous virtue lies surely in the fact that no more normal, average, decent-looking set of human beings could be found in the four kingdoms. The flashing eye, the arched brow, the nervous, sensitive hand—these would be unseemly and out of place here. The abnormal man would be pecked to death by all these cheerful sparrows. Look how irreverently they treat the Prime Minister himself. He has to submit to being questioned and cross-examined by a youth who seems to have rolled out of a punt on the river; or again to be heckled by a stubby little man who, to judge by his accent, must have been shovelling sugar into little blue bags behind a counter before he came to Westminster. Neither shows the least trace of fear or reverence. If the Prime Minister should one of these days turn into a statue, this apotheosis will not be reached here among the irreverent Commons.

All this time the fire of question and answer had popped and cracked incessantly; at last it stopped. The Secretary for Foreign Affairs rose, raised some typewritten sheets and read, clearly and firmly, a statement about some difficulty with Germany. He had seen the German Ambassador at the Foreign Office on Friday; he had said this, he had said that. He had crossed to Paris and seen M. Briand on Monday. They had agreed to this, they had suggested that. A plainer, a graver, a more business-like pronouncement could not be imagined. And as he spoke so directly, so firmly, a block of rough stone seemed to erect itself there on the Government benches. In other words, as one listened to the Secretary for Foreign Affairs endeavouring to guide our relations with Germany, it seemed clear that these ordinary-looking business-like men are responsible for acts which will remain when their red cheeks and top hats and check trousers are dust and ashes. Matters of great moment, which affect the happiness of people, the destinies of nations, are here at work chiselling and carving these very ordinary human beings. Down on this stuff of common humanity comes the stamp of a huge machine. And the machine itself and the man upon whom the stamp of the machine descends are both plain, featureless, impersonal.

Time was when the Foreign Secretary manipulated facts, toyed with them, elaborated them, and used all the resources of art and eloquence to make them appear what he chose they should appear to the people who had to accept his will. He was no common hard-worked man of business, with a small car and a villa and a great longing to get an afternoon off and play golf with his sons and daughters on a Surrey common. The Minister was once dressed to fit his part. Fulminations, perorations shook the air. Men were persuaded, juggled with, played upon. Pitt thundered; Burke was sublime. Individuality was allowed to unfold itself. Now no single human being can withstand the pressure of human affairs. They sweep over him and obliterate him; they leave him featureless, anonymous, their instrument merely. The conduct of affairs has passed from the hands of individuals to the hands of committees. Even committees can only guide them and hasten them and sweep them on to other committees. The intricacies and elegancies of personality are trappings that get in the way of business. The supreme need is despatch. A thousand ships come to anchor in the docks every week; how many thousand causes do not come daily to be decided in the House of Commons? Thus if statues are to be raised, they will become more and more monolithic, plain and featureless. They will cease to record Gladstone's collars, Dizzy's curl and Palmerston's wisp of straw. They will be like granite plinths set on the tops of moors to mark battles. The days of single men and personal power are over. Wit, invective, passion, are no longer called for. Mr. MacDonald is addressing not the small separate ears of his audience in the House of Commons, but men and women in factories, in shops, in farms on the veldt, in Indian villages. He is speaking to all men everywhere, not to us sitting here. Hence the clarity, the gravity, the plain impersonality of his statement. But if the days of the small separate statue are over, why should not the age of architecture dawn? That question asks itself as we leave the House of Commons. Westminster Hall raises its immense dignity as we pass out. Little men and women are moving soundlessly about the floor. They appear minute, perhaps pitiable; but also venerable and beautiful under the curve of the vast dome, under the perspective of the huge columns. One would rather like to be a small nameless animal in a vast cathedral. Let us rebuild the world then as a splendid hall; let us give up making statues and inscribing them with impossible virtues.

Let us see whether democracy which makes halls cannot surpass the aristocracy which carved statues. But there are still innumerable policemen. A blue giant stands at every door to see that we do not hurry on with our democracy too fast. "Admission is on Saturdays only between the hours of ten and twelve." That is the kind of notice that checks our dreaming progress. And must we not admit a distinct tendency in our corrupt mind soaked with habit to stop and think: "Here stood King Charles when they sentenced him to death; here the Earl of Essex; and Guy Fawkes; and Sir Thomas More." The mind, it seems, likes to perch, in its flight through empty space, upon some remarkable nose, some trembling hand; it loves the flashing eye, the arched brow, the abnormal, the particular, the splendid human

being. So let us hope that democracy will come, but only a hundred years hence, when we are beneath the grass; or that by some stupendous stroke of genius both will be combined, the vast hall and the small, the particular, the individual human being.

PORTRAIT OF

A LONDONER

Nobody can be said to know London who does not know one true Cockney—who cannot turn down a side street, away from the shops and the theatres, and knock at a private door in a street of private houses.

Private houses in London are apt to be much of a muchness. The door opens on a dark hall; from the dark hall rises a narrow staircase; off the landing opens a double drawing-room, and in this double drawing-room are two sofas on each side of a blazing fire, six armchairs, and three long windows giving upon the street. What happens in the back half of the drawing-room which looks upon the gardens of other houses is often a matter of considerable conjecture. But it is with the front drawing-room that we are here concerned; for Mrs. Crowe always sat there in an armchair by the fire; it was there that she had her being; it was there that she poured out tea.

That she was born in the country seems, though strange, to be a fact: that she sometimes left London, in those summer weeks when London ceases to be London, is also true. But where she went or what she did when she was out of London, when her chair was empty, her fire unlit and her table unlaid, nobody knew or could imagine. To figure Mrs. Crowe in her black dress and her veil and her cap, walking in a field among turnips or climbing a hill where cows were grazing, is beyond the scope of the wildest imagination.

There by the fire in winter, by the window in summer, she had sat for sixty years—but not alone. There was always some-one in the armchair opposite, paying a call. And before the first caller had been seated ten minutes the door always opened, and the maid Maria, she of the prominent eyes and prominent teeth, who had opened the door for sixty years, opened it once more and announced a second visitor; and then a third, and then a fourth.

A tete-a-tete with Mrs. Crowe was unknown. She disliked tete-a-tetes. It was part of a peculiarity that she shared with many hostesses that she was never specially intimate with any-one. For example, there was always an elderly man in the cor-ner by the cabinet—who seemed, indeed, as much a part of that admirable piece of eighteenth-century furniture as its own brass claws. But he was always addressed as Mr. Graham—never John, never William: though sometimes she would call him "dear Mr. Graham" as if to mark the fact that she had known him for sixty years.

The truth was she did not want intimacy; she wanted con-versation. Intimacy has a way of breeding silence, and silence she abhorred. There must be talk, and it must be general, and it must be about everything. It must not go too deep, and it must not be too clever, for if it went too far in either of these directions somebody was sure to feel out of it, and to sit balanc-ing his tea-cup, saying nothing.

Thus Mrs. Crowe's drawing-room had little in common with the celebrated salons of the memoir writers. Clever peo-ple often came there—judges, doctors, members of parlia-ment, writers, musicians, people who travelled, people who played polo, actors and complete nonentities, but if anyone said a brilliant thing it was felt to be rather a breach of etiquette—an accident that one ignored, like a fit of sneezing, or some catastrophe with a muffin. The talk that Mrs. Crowe liked and inspired was a glorified version of village gossip. The village was London, and the gossip was about London life. But Mrs. Crowe's great gift consisted in making the vast metropolis seem as small as a village with one church, one manor house and twenty-five cottages. She had first-hand information about every play, every picture show, every trial, every divorce case. She knew who was marrying, who was dying, who was in town and who was out. She would mention the fact that she had just seen Lady Umphleby's car go by, and hazard a guess that she was going to visit her daughter whose baby had been born last night, just as a village woman speaks of the Squire's lady driving to the station to meet Mr. John, who is expected down from town.

And as she had made these observations for the past fifty years or so, she had acquired an amazing store of information about the lives of other people. When Mr. Smedley, for instance, said that his daughter was engaged to Arthur Beecham, Mrs. Crowe at once remarked that in that case she would be a cousin twice removed to Mrs. Firebrace, and in a sense niece to Mrs. Burns, by her first marriage with Mr. Minchin of Blackwater Grange. But Mrs. Crowe was not in the least a snob. She was merely a collector of relationships; and her amazing skill in this direction served to give a family and domestic character to her gatherings, for it is surprising how many people are twentieth cousins, if they did but know it.

To be admitted to Mrs. Crowe's house was therefore to become the member of a club, and the subscription demanded was the payment of so many items of gossip every year. Many people's first thought when the house caught fire or the pipes burst or the housemaid decamped with the butler, must have been "I will run round and tell that to Mrs. Crowe." But here again distinctions had to be observed. Certain people had the right to run round at lunchtime; others, and these were the most numerous, must go between the hours of five and seven. The class who had the privilege of dining with Mrs. Crowe was a small one. Perhaps only Mr. Graham and Mrs. Burke actually dined with her, for she was not a rich woman. Her black dress was a trifle shabby; her diamond brooch was always the same diamond brooch. Her favourite meal was tea, because the tea-table can be supplied economically, and there is an elasticity about tea which suited her gregarious temper. But whether it was lunch or tea, the meal had a distinct character, just as a dress and her jewellery suited her to perfection and had a fashion of their own. There would be a special cake, a special pudding—something peculiar to the house and as much part of the establishment as Maria the old servant, or Mr. Graham the old friend, or the old chintz on the chair, or the old carpet on the floor.

That Mrs. Crowe must sometimes have taken the air, that she did sometimes become a guest at other people's luncheons and teas, is true. But in society she seemed furtive and fragmentary and incomplete, as if she had merely looked in at the wedding or the evening party or the funeral to pick up some scraps of news that she needed to complete her own hoard. Thus she was seldom induced to take a seat; she was always on the wing. She looked out of place among other people's chairs and tables; she must have her own chintzes and her own cabinet and her own Mr. Graham under it in order to be completely herself. As years went on these little raids into the outer world practically ceased. She had made her nest so compact and so complete that the outer world had not a feather or a twig to add to it. Her own cronies were so faithful, moreover, that she could trust them to convey any little piece of news that she ought to add to her collection. It was unnecessary that she should leave her own chair by the fire in winter, by the window in summer. And with the passage of years her knowledge became, not more profound—profundity was not her line—but more rounded, and more complete. Thus if a new play were a great success, Mrs. Crowe was able next day not merely to record the fact with a sprinkle of amusing gossip from behind the scenes, but she could cast back to other first nights, in the eighties, in the nineties, and describe what Ellen Terry had worn, what Duse had done, how dear Mr. Henry James had said—nothing very remarkable perhaps; but as she spoke it seemed as if all the pages of London life for fifty years past were being lightly shuffled for one's amusement. There were many; and the pictures on them were bright and brilliant and of famous people; but Mrs. Crowe by no means dwelt on the past—she by no means exalted it above the present.

Indeed, it was always the last page, the present moment that mattered most. The delightful thing about London was that it was always giving one something new to look at, something fresh to talk about. One only had to keep one's eyes open; to sit down in one's own chair from five to seven every day of the week. As she sat in her chair with her guests ranged round she would give from time to time a quick bird-like glance over her shoulder at the window, as if she had half an eye on the street, as if she had half an ear upon the cars and the omnibuses and the cries of the paper boys under the window. Why, something new might be happening this very moment. One could not spend too much time on the past: one must not give all one's attention to the present.

Nothing was more characteristic and perhaps a little disconcerting than the eagerness with which she would look up and break her sentence in the middle when the door opened and Maria, grown very portly and a little deaf, announced someone new. Who was about to enter? What had he or she got to add to the talk? But her deftness in extracting whatever might be their gift, her skill in throwing it into the common pool, were such that no harm was done; and it was part of her peculiar triumph that the door never opened too often; the circle never grew beyond her sway.

Thus, to know London not merely as a gorgeous spectacle, a mart, a court, a hive of industry, but as a place where people meet and talk, laugh, marry, and die, paint, write and act, rule and legislate, it was essential to know Mrs. Crowe. It was in her drawing-room that the innumerable fragments of the vast metropolis seemed to come together into one lively, comprehensible, amusing and agreeable whole. Travellers absent for years, battered and sun-dried men just landed from India or

Africa, from remote travels and adventures among savages and tigers, would come straight to the little house in the quiet street to be taken back into the heart of civilisation at one stride. But even London itself could not keep Mrs. Crowe alive for ever. It is a fact that one day Mrs. Crowe was not sitting in the armchair by the fire as the clock struck five; Maria did not open the door; Mr. Graham had detached himself from the cabinet. Mrs. Crowe is dead, and London—no, though London still exists, London will never be the same city again.